A
Shot
in the Light

REFLECTIONS DAY BY DAY

Michael Crawford

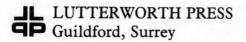

LUTTERWORTH PRESS
Guildford, Surrey

With love
To Sue, Graeme and Jill.

First published in 1981

Copyright © Michael Crawford 1981

ISBN 0-7188-2503-9

Photoset in 11/12 pt. Plantin by
Rowland Phototypesetting Limited, Bury St Edmunds, Suffolk
Printed in Great Britain by St Edmundsbury Press
Bury St Edmunds, Suffolk.

Introduction

I have found, and still find, the Bible a difficult book – difficult to read, difficult to understand. But I know that for anyone at all seriously interested in the Christian faith, this unique library of books which comprise the Bible – sixty-six of them, no less – is indispensable reading. And while that may just be a profound way of stating the obvious, it's still a challenging proposition. Paul's words on the primacy of Scripture immediately come to mind,

> All scripture is inspired by God and is useful for teaching the faith and correcting error, for re-setting the direction of a man's life and training him in good living. The scriptures are the comprehensive equipment of the man of God, and fit him fully for all branches of his work (2 Tim. 3:16, 17, JBP).

It all adds up to no mean challenge for minister or priest. Let the waters of application and resolve dry up here, and sooner rather than later there are big problems.

Reading the Bible requires a rare inner consistency of discipline. And if we clerics, the so-called professionals, find we are pushed all the way to do this very ordinary, and yet extraordinary work –

I have a shrewd feeling that I speak for many of us in this – what of the plain person who often simply hasn't the time, nor, let's be quite honest, the inclination to start digging with any real determination in the scriptural plot?

Perhaps it's a paradox that despite the large number of new translations, it seems that fewer and fewer people are reading the world's continuing bestseller. 'On the bookshelf of life, God is a useful work of reference, always at hand but seldom consulted' – so says Dag Hammarskjold in that very special diary of his, *Markings*. Yes, the Bible is there all right, safe and solid 'on the bookshelf of life'. But it has to be taken down. And dipped into. And it has to be read, fairly and squarely.

This book of readings – sacred and secular – is an attempt to get people looking at Scripture in what I hope is a fresh and different context. I do realise that the passages here are a quite personal and arbitrary selection – but a word about this context.

The minister's reading takes in Scripture and non-scriptural material, and the latter certainly includes books about the Bible, and articles and books that, in some ways, might appear to be very far removed from the world of faith. I have to admit for myself that sometimes the shadow of sheer obligation to read falls across the pages of the Bible. It's precisely then that secular reading can bring its own kind of light with its complete difference, relaxation, and recreation; and ultimately, for me, re-creation. Often it has been a source of delight and surprise to find that passages from 'outside' reading strike a scriptural chord in me. And while the secular passage has its own specialness, it still persuasively pushes me back to Scripture to bring into focus there the foundational passages that, in their own eternally contemporary way, have said it all before.

The secular passage has then been responsible for giving me a new incentive for a more resourceful examination of Scripture. But I also believe that the secular passage has its own inherent kind of integrity. And often that integrity is very close to holiness. Books like *Defeat into Victory* by Field-Marshal William Slim; *Delius – as I knew him* by Eric Fenby; *The Real Enemy* by Pierre d'Harcourt; and *Dietrich Bonhoeffer – Theologian, Christian, Contemporary* by Eberhard Bethge (passages from all these are included in this book of readings), have been milestones in my spiritual growth. They have gripped me. They have become part of me as I have tried to benefit from their many invaluable insights. They indirectly convince me of the preeminence and sheer indispensability of Scripture. They also convince me that the word of God certainly does not finish with the last great benediction in Revelation. That word has a disconcerting habit of subtly permeating the world and continues to speak cogently in the places where sometimes we would least expect it. If then on occasion, I find, Bible-reading becoming irksome, I also find that, due to the deft intervention of some random extract from secular reading, I am enabled to return to Scripture with a newly-awakened verve and vitality.

What I have done in *A Shot in the Light* is to start off each day of one month with a passage which comes from secular reading – and that covers a multitude of sources: books, magazines, newspapers, and even a note from a record-sleeve. All of these have said something very definite to me and all in their own way have propelled me irresistibly towards the Bible. That rings a bell – when did I hear that before? When and where does Scripture say something similar to this? When does it say it differently? Or definitively? The passage from book or newspaper is then followed by the scriptural passage which is the apposite one for me. Sometimes Scripture echoes exactly the spirit of the secular passage; sometimes it disagrees and sets up its own kind of internal friction; sometimes it corrects; sometimes it spells out the eternal dimension; sometimes it complements (and compliments!); and sometimes the world of Scripture seems at one and the same time to be both far and near to the meaning and spirit of the original.

I hope the reader finds the original passage stimulating and eventful in its own right. I hope the reader finds that the very personal passages of Scripture have a 'fresh immediacy' to them. I hope most of all that a kind of positive tension is generated between the secular and sacred passages, and, that as a result of this, the reader will be prepared to read in and around the selected texts and passages, and even begin to make deeper forays into the fascinating terrain of the Bible.

It seemed right that in selecting the passages of Scripture a mixture of both old and new was called for. Accordingly there is a blend – most of the passages are from *The New English Bible* with all its terseness and pace; some passages come from *The New Testament in Modern English* by J. B. Phillips – here there's a splendid lucidity in a most contemporary style; and not to include some of the passages which give the full flavour of the 'unbridled magnificence' of the Authorised Version would surely be a mistake.

Secular passages and then passages and texts from Scripture – that is the order. And to round things off I have added, for the most part, short reflections, meditations, and prayers.

Most of the material in this short book has 'lived' before in worship. It is my hope that it can 'live' again on the printed page.

Acknowledgements

The author and publisher wish to thank the following publishers, copyright owners and authors for permission to use their material.

William Collins Sons & Company Limited, *The New Testament in Modern English*, J. B. Phillips (JBP).

The New English Bible, second edition © 1970, by permission of Oxford and Cambridge University Presses (NEB).

Extracts from the Authorized Version of the Bible, which is Crown Copyright, are used with permission (AV).

The Hogarth Press Ltd., *Journey into Russia*, *The Lost World of the Kalahari*, Laurens van der Post.

Angus & Robertson Ltd., *Duet for Three Hands*, Cyril Smith.

Cassell Ltd., *Defeat into Victory*, Field-Marshal Sir William Slim.

Times Newspapers Limited, *The Making of a Critic*, Sir Harold Hobson.

Longman, *The Real Enemy*, Pierre d'Harcourt.

Faber and Faber Ltd., *Markings*, Dag Hammarskjold translated by W. H. Auden and Lief Sjoberg.

Eric Fenby, *Delius – as I knew him*.

United Nations, *Apartheid in Practice*, Prof. Leslie Rubin.

Hart-Davis MacGibbon Ltd./Granada Publishing Ltd., *The Greatest: My Own Story*, Muhammad Ali with Richard Durham.

The Scotsman, 14 January 1977, 18 October, 1971, 31 January 1975 (Days 10, 11, 15).

Victor Gollancz and Sphere Books Ltd., *Emma and I*, Sheila Hocken.

EMI Limited and Andre Previn for sleeve notes on Rachmaninov, Symphony No. 2.

The International Festival of Youth Orchestras and the Performing Arts and The Rt. Hon. Edward Heath for his welcoming address to the Festival in the Festival Brochure of 1980.

The Sunday Times Special Projects Unit wall chart *Indians of the North American Plains* (Days 16 and 30).

The *Observer* for extracts from articles by Patrick O'Donovan and Sir John Hunt.

Hamish Hamilton Ltd., *Farewell Recital*, Gerald Moore.

William Collins, Sons & Company Limited, *Dietrich Bonhoeffer – Theologian: Christian: Contemporary*, Eberhard Bethge.

Systems Publications Limited, 'X-Rays', *The New Caxton Encyclopedia*.

Tavistock Publications Ltd., *Aggression on the Road*, Meyer Parry.

Hodder & Stoughton Ltd., *M.C.C. – The Autobiography of a Cricketer*, Colin Cowdrey.

Hamish Hamilton Limited, *The Plague (La Peste)*, Albert Camus, copyright © by Albert Camus, translation

A shot in the light

(Laurens van der Post in The Lost World of the Kalahari *– a fascinating account of his independent expedition in search of the Bushmen of the Kalahari desert – relates a particular incident which befell the expedition when it was in the Swamp of Despond, deep in the Kalahari. Critically short of food van der Post and two companions go off on a desperate hunt for game. A lechwe (kind of antelope) is sighted, but it becomes increasingly difficult for the hunters to take up an advantageous position from which they could attempt to make the kill.)*

The lechwe, uneasy, stood between us and the light, up to its pointed chin in reeds, and looking hard in our direction. It was my last chance to shoot, but so forlorn a chance that it was hardly worth taking. I reckoned the distance was a hundred and fifty yards; the visible target an elegant head and a bit of smooth slim throat; the direction almost straight into a sun level with the eye. If I had not been so convinced of the absolute necessity of getting meat for the camp I would not have attempted it for fear of wounding the lechwe.

. . . In my hands was the new gun which I had bought because of my wife's insistence. I had not yet fired at a live target, though, of course, I had zeroed it on a marked one. I said a wordless prayer to the unknown gods of the world around me and aimed at the living target. As soon as I had the lechwe within my sights I shot quickly without deliberation and as much from instinct as from observation. As the harp-like silence fled swiftly from the day, the lechwe vanished instantly in the long reeds. I was certain I had missed, but my two companions were shouting, 'Oh! Our master. Oh! Our father. You've hit it. Lo! The lechwe is dead!'

'No,' I told them, 'it was an impossible shot. I think I've only frightened it and it's off round that mound.'

Yet, when we waded through the water now red with the sacrifice of day, we found the lechwe shot through the middle of its long throat, the bone of the neck so cleanly broken that there was no look of pain on its delicate face. Its coat was golden with warmth and its long magnetic toes were still coming, trembling together. Yet I had no regret at so needful a killing. Indeed I felt a profound gratitude to the animal and life that I had been allowed to provide food for so many hungry men.

God said, 'Let the earth bring forth living creatures, according to their kind: cattle, reptiles, and wild animals, all according to their kind.' So it was; God made wild animals, cattle, and all reptiles, each according to its kind; and he saw that it was good. Then God said, 'Let us make man in our image and likeness to rule the fish in the sea, the birds of heaven, the cattle, all wild animals on earth, and all reptiles that crawl upon the earth.' So God created man in his own image; in the image of God he created him; male and female he created them. God blessed them and said to them, 'Be fruitful and increase, fill the earth and subdue it, rule over the fish in the sea, the birds of heaven, and every living thing that moves upon the earth.'

(Genesis 1:24–28, NEB)

Almighty God, for the wonder and sparkle of nature, for the rippling muscles of the animal kingdom, for the crown of your creation, mankind, we thank you.
Help us to put on the shoes of reverence, the clothes of thankfulness, and to have firmly in our hands the staff of reality – as we make the great pilgrimage through a still beautiful and majestic world, our world, your world. Amen.

DAY 2

Practice makes perfect

A professional musician must, of course, come to terms with life and realise that he can never really reach ultimate perfection; otherwise he will be a bitterly unhappy man. However, the business of trying to get there should absorb his interest, and in the meantime he does at least produce some beauty.

(Cyril Smith in his book *Duet for Three Hands*.)

No, you are to be perfect like your Heavenly Father.

(Matthew 5:48, JBP)

God has given me that genuine righteousness which comes from faith in Christ. How changed are my ambitions! Now I long to know Christ and the power shown by his resurrection: now I long to share his sufferings, even to die as he died, so that I may perhaps attain as he did, the resurrection from the dead. Yet, my brothers, I do not consider myself to have "arrived" spiritually, nor do I consider myself already perfect. But I keep going on, grasping ever more firmly that purpose for which Christ grasped me.

(Philippians 3:9b–12, JBP)

Father,
Are we meant to scale the pinnacles of perfection?
Or are we simply meant to try our hardest to get there?
And the true virtue is in the trying.
What is perfection?
Being complete?
And what exactly is meant by that?
Do we become complete when we make the perfect acceptance of our own incompleteness?

Let us, like Paul, have the gumption 'to keep going on'.
Let us strive to realise our best.
And let us seek to be more well-rounded and mature in our openness to others, and in the total strategy of our living.

DAY 3

Right priorities

(The epic Defeat into Victory *by Field-Marshal Sir William Slim gives a vivid account of how, in the 2nd World War, the Japanese forces were eventually driven out of Burma. But when Slim first took command of the newly-formed 14th Army in 1943 the outlook was bleak. The Japanese forces had carried all before them and Slim realised only too well that facing him and his men were many daunting problems. They all added up to three major anxieties – the lack of supplies, ill-health, and low morale. In* Defeat into Victory *Slim soon realised that if firm foundations were to be built for recapturing the initiative from the enemy, certain clear priorities had first to be established – and number one on the list was morale.)*

So when I took command, I sat quietly down to work out this business of morale. I came to certain conclusions, based not on any theory that I had studied, but on some experience and a good deal of hard thinking. It was on these conclusions that I set out consciously to raise the fighting spirit of my army.

Morale is a state of mind. It is that intangible force which will move a whole group of men to give their last ounce to achieve something, without counting the cost to themselves; that makes them feel they are part of something greater than themselves. If they are to feel that, their morale must, if it is to endure – and the essence of morale is that it should endure – have certain foundations. These foundations are spiritual, intellectual, and material, and that is the order of their importance. Spiritual first, because only spiritual foundations can stand real strain. Next intellectual, because men are swayed by reason as well as feeling. Material last – important, but last – because the very highest kinds of morale are often met when material conditions are lowest.

Full of the Holy Spirit, Jesus returned from the Jordan, and for forty days was led by the Spirit up and down the wilderness and tempted by the devil.

All that time he had nothing to eat, and at the end of it he was famished. The devil said to him, 'If you are the Son of God, tell this stone to become bread.' Jesus answered, 'Scripture says, "Man cannot live on bread alone." '

(Luke 4:1–4, NEB)

Therefore, take up God's armour; then you will be able to stand your ground when things are at their worst, to complete every task and still to stand. Stand firm, I say. Buckle on the belt of truth; for coat of mail put on integrity; let the shoes on your feet be the gospel of peace, to give you firm footing; and, with all these, take up the great shield of faith, with which you will be able to quench all the flaming arrows of the evil one. Take salvation for helmet; for sword, take that which the Spirit gives you – the words that come from God.

(Ephesians 6:13–17, NEB)

Take time and trouble to keep yourself spiritually fit. Bodily fitness has a certain value, but spiritual fitness is essential both for this present life and for the life to come. There is no doubt about this at all, and Christians should remember it. It is because we realise the paramount importance of the spiritual that we labour and struggle. We place our whole confidence in the living God, the saviour of all men, and particularly of those who believe in him. These convictions should be the basis of your instruction and teaching.

(1 Timothy 4:7b–10, JBP)

Man cannot live on bread alone. Nor can he live without it, Father.
So we give thanks for the staff of life – bread for ourselves, and the challenge of bread for others. We thank you for the sustenance of mind and spirit, and for the food of unselfish love and encouragement. Above all we give thanks for the bread of self-giving we have in Jesus Christ.
Help us to follow him with that strong trinity of body, mind, and soul. Amen.

Critic's credo

(Sir Harold Hobson, the distinguished ex-drama critic of the Sunday Times, *succinctly spells out his credo as a critic.)*

What I heard in the Christian Science Church as a boy has governed my attitude to drama.

In that Church, I heard week after week a school-master, Arthur Allen, read from the Bible with a splendour and a beauty that made me realise for the first time that the human voice joined to great words can be an instrument of supernal splendour. When Mr. Allen read: 'Whatsoever things are honest, whatsoever things are true . . . if there be *any* virtue, and if there be *any* praise, think on these things,' he made on me an indelible impression, and I have always gone into the theatre with the determination to find in a play, if it were possible, delight and excitement rather than defect and boredom. On that resolution my whole professional career was built.

Finally, brethren, whatsoever things are true, whatsoever things are honest, whatsoever things are just, whatsoever things are pure, whatsoever things are lovely, whatsoever things are of good report; if there be any virtue, and if there be any praise, think on these things. Those things, which ye have both learned, and received, and heard, and seen in me, do: and the God of peace shall be with you.

(Philippians 4:8, 9, AV)

Father, help us to achieve a wholesome and positive attitude towards our world.
Help us to look for the bracing and constructive things in life, and yet not to become totally unrealistic and hopelessly naive in the whole process.

A genius for serving

(Pierre d'Harcourt in his very moving and inspiring book, The Real Enemy, *recounts his harrowing experiences in the Buchenwald concentration camp in the last war. Here, like a gleam of light in the darkness, he tells us about one of Buchenwald's authentic latter-day saints.)*

I still recall my sense of revulsion when I saw M. He was a stage caricature of the most effeminate type of homosexual. His walk, his figure, his manner were all unbelievably grotesque. He was of more than medium height and not badly built, but his mincing gait and gestures made him look smaller and slighter. His face was womanish without being in the least attractive. It was broad, squat and Asiatic, with empty, characterless eyes. The only feature about him that did not repel was his voice, which was that of a very cultivated man. He came from an ancient Rumanian family, and had been a horticulturist and had specialised in roses. He was a sincere and profound Roman Catholic. Now, in the little camp, he had shown where his true genius lay. It was to care more for the most wretched and degraded sick human beings than for himself. Month after month he fetched and carried water, medicine, food or bowls of soup; he would sit and hold a dying man's hand while he gasped out his final prayers. He became one of the legends of Buchenwald in his own lifetime. He saved many lives, including my brother's, by his ministrations. And although he lived in the deepest of filth and disease for more than two years, he survived.

Look to each other's interests and not merely to your own. Let your bearing towards one another arise out of your life in Christ Jesus. For the divine nature was his from the first; yet he did not think to snatch at equality with God, but made himself nothing, assuming the nature of a slave. Bearing the human likeness, revealed in human shape, he humbled himself, and in obedience accepted even death – death on a cross.

(Philippians 2:4–9, NEB)

Jesus called them to him and said, 'You know that in the world the recognized rulers lord it over their subjects, and their great men make them feel the weight of authority. That is not the way with you; among you, whoever wants to be great must be your servant, and whoever wants to be first must be the willing slave of all. For even the Son of Man did not come to be served but to serve, and to give up his life as a ransom for many.'

(Mark 10:42–45, NEB)

During supper, Jesus, well aware that the Father had entrusted everything to him, and that he had come from God and was going back to God, rose from table, laid aside his garments, and taking a towel, tied it round him. Then he poured water into a basin, and began to wash his disciples' feet and to wipe them with the towel.

. . . After washing their feet and taking his garments again, he sat down. 'Do you understand what I have done for you?' he asked. 'You call me "Master" and "Lord", and rightly so, for that is what I am. Then if I, your Lord and Master, have washed your feet, you also ought to wash one another's feet. I have set you an example: you are to do as I have done for you.'

(John 13: 2–5, 12–14, NEB)

The world tells us that it's the step up that counts; but the Christ firmly and quite unmistakably takes a step down in the world, so that we won't miss the primacy of serving.
Give us, Father, the willingness to live for others, so that something of your hope and healing may flow through us and give new life to those in need.

Affirmative!

(The following three lines come from Dag Ham-marskjold's remarkable Markings – *a diary with a difference. Dag Hammarskjold was Secretary-General of the United Nations from 1953 to his untimely death in 1961.* Markings *is a unique spiritual record of one very public, and yet very private man's journey through life. Henry P. van Dusen in* Dag Hammarskjold – a Biographical Interpretation of Markings *points out that this entry was made just before he accepted the formidable challenge of the Secretary-Generalship of the United Nations.)*

> – Night is drawing nigh –
> For all that has been – Thanks!
> To all that shall be – Yes!

But I do concentrate on this: I leave the past behind and with hands out-stretched to whatever lies ahead I go straight for the goal – my reward the honour of my high calling by God in Christ Jesus.

(Philippians 3:13b, 14, JBP)

Lord, let the response be clear and firm, Yes! To you, to life, and to all that it brings us. Amen!

The irresistible call

(The young musician, Eric Fenby, in his book Delius – as I knew him, *recounts how he first came to be interested in the music of Frederick Delius, but, more than that, how he was strangely moved by the composer's seemingly hopeless situation.)*

About this time I had read several articles on Delius and his music, and had learnt of his unhappy plight, namely that he was now blind and paralysed and unable to work any more. But the real tragedy of it all, or so it seemed to me, was to hear that the composer was worried and unhappy because it was physically impossible for him to continue and finish his life's work. Apparently there were several works which he had begun, and been unable to complete. He could bear with his misfortunes if only he could finish these scores.

To have something beautiful in you and not be able to bring it to fruition because the human machinery had broken down seemed hard. To be a genius as this man plainly was, and have something beautiful in you and not be able to rid yourself of it because you could no longer see your score paper and no longer hold your pen – well, the thought was unbearable!

I remember how, with my dog, Peter, I walked for miles one stormy day on the cliffs reflecting on the helplessness and misery of the man. What delicacy of feeling was in his music! What must such a sensitive nature be suffering? Could not anything be done? Of course, I would be willing to . . . But how dare I presume such a thing! It was preposterous! Ashamed and surprised, I dismissed the idea from my mind and, battling with the wind, tried to think of other things.

During the next few weeks the conceit that I could help became an obsession. It chased me like some Hound of Heaven, and I hid from it under any and every excuse that I could find; but it was always there, and in the end I could not sleep for it. Finally it conquered me, and, getting up in the middle of the night, I took pen and paper and wrote to Delius offering my help for three or four years. I would do anything to be the means of his finishing that music, and, provided that my suggestion was acceptable to him at all, I felt certain that I would succeed in my purpose. How it was going to be done – well, God alone knew the answer to that!

(*Eric Fenby's offer of help was warmly accepted. He left Scarborough in October 1928 and travelled to Grez-sur-Loing in France where Delius lived. Slowly and laboriously an effective working relationship was built up between the irascible Delius and young Fenby, and the happy result was an Indian Summer for Delius, and the completion of some of his finest work.*)

So the child Samuel was in the Lord's service under his master Eli. Now in those days the word of the Lord was seldom heard, and no vision was granted. But one night, Eli, whose eyes were dim and his sight failing, was lying down in his usual place, while Samuel slept in the temple of the Lord where the Ark of God was. Before the lamp of God had gone out, the Lord called him, and Samuel answered, 'Here I am', and ran to Eli saying, 'You called me: here I am.' 'No, I did not call you,' said Eli; 'lie down again.' So he went and lay down. The Lord called Samuel again, and he got up and went to Eli. 'Here I am,' he said; 'surely you called me.' 'I did not call, my son,' he answered; 'lie down again.' Now Samuel had not yet come to know the Lord, and the word of the Lord had not been disclosed to him. When the Lord called him for the third time, he again went to Eli and said, 'Here I am; you did call me.' Then Eli understood that it was the Lord calling the child; he told Samuel to go and lie down and said, 'If he calls again, say, "Speak, Lord; thy servant hears thee." ' So Samuel went and lay down in his place.

The Lord came and stood there, and called, 'Samuel, Samuel', as before. Samuel answered, 'Speak; thy servant hears thee.' The Lord said, 'Soon I shall do something in Israel which will ring in the ears of all who hear it. When that day comes I will make good every word I have spoken against Eli and his family from beginning to end. You are to tell him that my judgement on his house shall stand for ever because he knew of his sons' blasphemies against God and did not rebuke them.

Therefore I have sworn to the family of Eli that their abuse of sacrifices and offerings shall never be expiated.'

Samuel lay down till morning and then opened the doors of the house of the Lord, but he was afraid to tell Eli about the vision. Eli called Samuel: 'Samuel, my son', he said; and he answered, 'Here I am.' Eli asked, 'What did the Lord say to you? Do not hide it from me. God forgive you if you hide one word of all that he said to you.' Then Samuel told him everything and hid nothing. Eli said, 'The Lord must do what is good in his eyes.'

As Samuel grew up, the Lord was with him, and none of his words went unfulfilled. From Dan to Beersheba, all Israel recognized that Samuel was confirmed as a prophet of the Lord.

(1 Samuel 3:1–20, NEB)

During the night a vision came to Paul: a Macedonian stood there appealing to him and saying, 'Come across to Macedonia and help us.' After he had seen this vision we set about getting a passage to Macedonia, concluding that God had called us to bring them the good news.

(Acts 16:9, 10, NEB)

Lord, when we would far rather sleep, let that persistent 'still small voice' wake us up!

A fundamental unity

(*The following is from* Apartheid in Practice, Section eleven – Race and Colour, Statement No. 206. *This study has been prepared by Professor Leslie Rubin at the request of the United Nations Centre against Apartheid, formerly the Unit on Apartheid. In* Apartheid in Practice *Professor Rubin formulates 300 statements which give the distilled essence of the many and complex South African race laws – Apartheid. Leslie Rubin is Professor of Comparative Law at Howard University in America, and prior to that, was a Senator in South Africa representing African voters.*)

A white person is 'a person who (a) in appearance obviously is a white person and who is not generally accepted as a coloured person, or (b) is generally accepted as a white person, and is not in appearance obviously NOT a white person but even a person whose appearance is white and who has been accepted as white will not be so classified if one of his natural parents has been classified as a member of another race.'

There is no such thing as Jew and Greek, slave and freeman, male and female; for you are all one person in Christ Jesus.

(Galatians 3:28, NEB)

In this new man of God's design there is no distinction between Greek and Hebrew, Jew or Gentile, foreigner or savage, slave or free man. Christ is all that matters for Christ lives in them all.

(Colossians 3:11, JBP)

Black and white,
White and black,
Colours so clear and defined,
Yet lending themselves to inaccuracy, fear, and division:
Because people are not really black, nor are they actually white –
People are pink and brown, chocolate and yellow and bronze.
But still the divisions remain.
So rejoice in red, the red of affirmation, the red of solidarity:
Because underneath the varied hues of skin,
Pumps the common red of mankind's blood –
Strong, and satisfying, and supreme!

DAY 9

The greatest

(Muhammad Ali holds court to the press after his predicted defeat of Sonny Liston in a World Heavyweight Fight.)

When it's all over, there's one final talk I want to make – to the press. When they gather in front of me, it's hard to forget that nearly all of them had considered me a hoax. They start to shoot questions at me, but I cut them off: 'Hold it! Hold it!' I say. 'You've all had chance to say what you thought before the fight. Now it's my turn. You all said Sonny Liston would kill me. You said he was better than Jack Johnson or Jack Dempsey, even Joe Louis, and you ranked them the best heavyweights of all time. You kept writing how Liston whipped Floyd Patterson twice, and when I told you I would get Liston in eight, you wouldn't believe it. Now I want all of you to tell the whole world while all the cameras are on us, tell the world that I'm The Greatest.'

There's a silence. 'Who's The Greatest?' I ask them. Nobody answers. They look down at their pads and microphones. 'Who's the Greatest?' I say again. They look up with solemn faces, but the room is still silent.

29

'For the LAST TIME!' I shout. 'All the eyes of the world on us. You just a bunch of hypocrites. I told you I was gonna get Liston and I got him. All the gamblers had me booked eight-to-one underdog. I proved all of you wrong. I shook up the world! Tell me who's the Greatest! WHO IS THE GREATEST?'

They hesitate for a minute, and finally in a dull tone they all answer, 'You are.'

These are the words of the Lord:
    Let not the wise man boast of his wisdom
      nor the valiant of his valour;
    let not the rich man boast of his riches;
    but if any man would boast, let him boast of this,
    that he understands and knows me.
    For I am the Lord, I show unfailing love,
    I do justice and right upon the earth;
    for on these I have set my heart.

(Jeremiah 9:23–24a, NEB)

A dispute arose among them: which of them was the greatest? Jesus knew what was passing in their minds, so he took a child by the hand and stood him at his side, and said, 'Whoever receives this child in my name receives me; and whoever receives me receives the One who sent me. For the least among you all – he is the greatest.'

(Luke 9:46–48, NEB)

But if there is to be bravado (and here I speak as a fool), I can indulge in it too. Are they Hebrews? So am I. Israelites? So am I. Abraham's descendants?

So am I. Are they servants of Christ? I am mad to speak like this, but I can outdo them. More over-worked than they, scourged more severely, more often imprisoned, many a time face to face with death. Five times the Jews have given me the thirty-nine strokes; three times I have been beaten with rods; once I was stoned; three times I have been shipwrecked, and for twenty-four hours I was adrift on the open sea. I have been constantly on the road; I have met dangers from rivers, dangers from robbers, dangers from my fellow-countrymen, dangers from foreigners, dangers in towns, dangers in the country, dangers at sea, dangers from false friends. I have toiled and drudged, I have often gone without sleep; hungry and thirsty, I have often gone fasting; and I have suffered from cold and exposure.

Apart from these external things, there is the responsibility that weighs on me every day, my anxious concern for all our congregations. If any-one is weak, do I not share his weakness? If anyone is made to stumble, does not my heart blaze with indignation? If boasting there must be, I will boast of the things that show up my weakness.

(2 Corinthians 11:21b–30, NEB)

Almighty God, grant us a confident humility, and a humble confidence in our own abilities.
But save us, at the same time, from that false modesty, which, by encouraging us to keep our strong points in low profile, only enables us to live below the level of our best. Amen.

Back garden star find

A postman and amateur astronomer has discovered a star using a small "very crude" telescope set up in his back garden. The discovery by Mr. Graham Hosty (27), of Blackmoorfoot Road, Crossland Moor, Huddersfield, has been confirmed by the International Astronomical Union.

He is only the second Briton in fifteen years to spot a "nova". "It is like winning the pools," said Mr. Hosty yesterday. "I am really excited about the find and I spent two sleepless nights waiting to hear confirmation."

"I set out to attempt to discover a nova about six months ago but I never thought it would happen – not so quickly anyway," he said.

The star is located in the constellation of Sagitta and will be entered in the astronomical catalogues as "Nova Sagitta 1977" along with the name of the discoverer.

(From *The Scotsman*)

But if from there you seek the Lord your God, you will find him, if indeed you search with all your heart and soul. When you are in distress and all these things come upon you, you will in days to come turn back to the Lord your God and obey him. The Lord your God is a merciful god; he will never fail you nor destroy you, nor will he forget the covenant guaranteed by oath with your forefathers.

Search into days gone by, long before your time, beginning at the day when God created man on earth; search from one end of heaven to the other, and ask if any deed as mighty as this has been seen or heard.

(Deuteronomy 4:29–32, NEB)

If you invoke me and pray to me, I will listen to you: when you seek me, you shall find me; if you search with all your heart, I will let you find me, says the Lord.

(Jeremiah 29:12–14a, NEB)

. . . seek, and you will find . . .

(Luke 11:9b, NEB)

Almighty God, our Father in Heaven, grant us the common grace of determination to keep on asking the relevant questions about life and faith; and to persevere in seeking for the solid things that give our lives purpose and ultimate meaning.

DAY 11

Beatification

Pope Paul today beatified a Polish priest who gave his life in a Nazi concentration camp for a fellow inmate – a man who survived to weep and shake with sobs today as he witnessed the solemn ceremony.

The Pope proclaimed Father Maximilian Kolbe as the first victim of the Nazi death camps to be inscribed in the rolls of the 'blessed'.

The Pontiff – the first to officiate at a beatification ceremony – said in an address to the 25,000 congregation that Father Kolbe was 'perhaps the brightest and most glittering figure' to emerge from the darkness of the Nazi epoch.

Seated in a place of honour near the altar was Auschwitz prisoner number 5659, a former Polish Army sergeant, Mr Franciszek Gajowniczek, whom Father Kolbe volunteered to replace in the starvation cells.

Father Kolbe asked to replace him because Mr Gajowniczek had a wife and children. Three weeks later, the priest was killed with a carbolic acid injection as he lay naked in an underground cell.

Mr Gajowniczek, who survived 5½ years at Auschwitz as four million Poles, Jews, and other Europeans were gassed and cremated, was the man chosen to carry to the altar and place in Pope Paul's hands the sacred hosts used during today's Mass.

The Pope smiled and leaned forward to embrace him as Mr Gajowniczek led the procession up the steps. The ex-sergeant, now silver-haired, and seventy years old, sobbed and clutched a handkerchief to his face as Polish hymns from the 4000 Poles present rang through St. Peter's, and the formal petition for Father Kolbe's beatification was read out in Polish.

(From *The Scotsman*)

There is no greater love than this, that a man should lay down his life for his friends.

(John 15:13, NEB)

Even for a just man one of us would hardly die, though perhaps for a good man one might actually brave death; but Christ died for us while we were yet sinners, and that is God's own proof of his love towards us.

(Romans 5:7, NEB)

It is by this that we know what love is: that Christ laid down his life for us. And we in our turn are bound to lay down our lives for our brothers.

(1 John 3:16, NEB)

Father,
loving you,
loving our neighbour
— and all men are our neighbours —
takes us unerringly to the heart of Christianity;
and for those precious self-sacrificing souls,
it takes them to the Cross itself.
We salute them.

I can see!

(Sheila Hocken, blind from early childhood, re-counts, in her inspiring Emma and I, *what it's like facing the challenges of blindness. Later on in the book, who should pad into her life but the beloved Emma, her faithful Labrador guide-dog and in-separable companion. Then comes the dramatic news that a particular operation might just conceiv-ably restore her sight. Sheila Hocken decides to take full advantage of this great opportunity. She enters hospital and a gifted surgeon performs the delicate operation. But will it be successful?)*

Then the bandages were off, and even then I did not know the result, because I had my eyes tight shut. I heard Sister saying, 'Come on, Sheila, open your eyes, the bandages are off . . .' And I gripped the armrests even harder, and opened my eyes.

What happened then – the only way I can de-scribe the sensation – is that I was suddenly hit, physically struck by brilliance, like an immense electric shock into my brain, and through my entire body. It flooded my whole being with a shock-wave, this utterly unimaginable, incandescent brightness: there was white in front of me, a daz-zling white that I could hardly bear to take in, and a vivid blue that I had never thought possible. It was

37

fantastic, marvellous, incredible. It was like the beginning of the world.

Then I turned and looked the other way, and there were greens, lots and lots of different greens, different shades, all quite unbelievable, and at the same time with this brilliance there flooded in sound, the sound of voices saying, 'Can you see, can you see?' But I was just so overwhelmed and spellbound by the sensation that had occupied every bit of me, as if the sun itself had burst into my brain and body and scattered every molten particle of its light and colour, that it took me some time to say anything. I looked back at the blue and said, 'Oh, it's blue, it's so beautiful.'

'It's me,' said Sister, coming towards me. The blue I could see was her uniform and she came right up to me and touched me, and said, 'Sheila, can you see it?' But I was still not coherent, and turned away, and said, 'Green, it's wonderful.' And this was Annette, and Linda, and Ann, who had gathered round me, and said, 'It's us, it's our uniforms.'

Then they realised I could see properly, because there was something away to the left that appeared to me a sort of yellow colour. I did not know what it was and said, 'What's that over there, that yellow thing?' And they said, 'It's a lamp, and it's really cream colour, pale cream.' But they knew for certain I could see it, though I had not known it was a lamp, and I had got the colour wrong. My memory of colours was pretty murky, but I could still identify the strongest ones. But until that moment in my life I had no idea that there could possibly exist so many clear, washed colours.

All this, I know, took only a few seconds. Everything crowded in. Then, just as quickly, everything started to go misty and blurred. The colours began to fade, and merge into one another, and I thought, 'No, oh no, it's going. That's all there's going to be, I can't bear it . . .' I was struck by sudden terror, and put my hands instinctively up to my eyes – and found there were tears streaming down my face. I thought, 'Oh, thank goodness, it's not going, it's just the tears.' And I wept uncontrollably, and could not stop, because of the joy and the shock that I still could not fully take in, as, at the same time, everyone round me, Sister, nurses, and all sorts of people I did not know, were shaking my hand – and I could just see enough to realise that they, too, were crying, and could not say anything for tears.

The memory of those few seconds is indelible; the sudden wonder, the sense of disbelief, yet belief, the engulfing knowledge that I could see. I could see!

As he went on his way Jesus saw a man blind from his birth. His disciples put the question, 'Rabbi, who sinned, this man or his parents? Why was he born blind?' 'It is not that this man or his parents sinned,' Jesus answered; 'he was born blind so that God's power might be displayed in curing him. While daylight lasts we must carry on the work of him who sent me; night comes, when no one can work. While I am in the world I am the

39

light of the world.'

With these words he spat on the ground and made a paste with the spittle; he spread it on the man's eyes, and said to him, 'Go and wash in the pool of Siloam.' (The name means 'sent'.) The man went away and washed, and when he returned he could see.

His neighbours and those who were accustomed to see him begging said, 'Is not this the man who used to sit and beg?' Others said, 'Yes, this is the man.' Others again said, 'No, but it is someone like him.' The man himself said, 'I am the man.' They asked him, 'How were your eyes opened?' He replied, 'The man called Jesus made a paste and smeared my eyes with it, and told me to go to Siloam and wash. I went and washed, and gained my sight.' 'Where is he?' they asked. He answered, 'I do not know.'

The man who had been blind was brought before the Pharisees. As it was a Sabbath day when Jesus made the paste and opened his eyes, the Pharisees now asked him by what means he had gained his sight. The man told them, 'He spread a paste on my eyes; then I washed, and now I can see.' Some of the Pharisees said, 'This fellow is no man of God; he does not keep the Sabbath.' Others said, 'How could such signs come from a sinful man?' So they took different sides. Then they continued to question him: 'What have you to say about him? It was your eyes he opened.' He answered, 'He is a prophet.'

The Jews would not believe that the man had been blind and had gained his sight, until they had summoned his parents and questioned them: 'Is this man your son? Do you say he was born blind? How is it that he can see now?' The parents replied, 'We know that he is our son, and that he was born blind. But how it is that he can now see, or who opened his eyes, we do not know. Ask him; he is of age; he will speak for himself.' His parents gave this answer because they were afraid of the Jews; for the Jewish authorities had already agreed that anyone who acknowledged Jesus as Messiah should be banned from the synagogue. That is why the parents said, 'He is of age; ask him.'

So for the second time they summoned the man who had been blind, and said, 'Speak the truth before God. We know that this fellow is a sinner.' 'Whether or not he is a sinner, I do not know', the man replied. 'All I know is this: once I was blind, now I can see.'

(John 9:1–25, NEB)

Almighty God, thank you for eyes –
  eyes to see the wonder of creation,
  eyes to see the sparkle of a smile,
  eyes to see your goodness.
Forgive us when we look at our world and see decay,
cruelty, malice, and the 'tyranny of change'.
Give us that penetrating gaze, so that we can see –
  the inner fires of good-will and beneficence; generosity
  the strong light of righteousness;
  and the mellow sun of unselfish love warming our
  chilled and dispirited world.
Give us eyes to – SEE!

DAY 13

Just an ordinary orange

(Andre Previn writes the following in a record-sleeve note to Rachmaninov's Symphony No. 2 – the complete version – EMI Records, ASD 2889 Stereo.)

The London Symphony Orchestra and I have been playing this particular symphony for a long time, and in a great many places. We've given performances throughout Europe, the United States, the Far East, and in Russia, and no matter how otherwise disparate the local culture or history, Rachmaninov's passionate music reached out to every listener.

One of the most unforgettable events of my musical life was seeing members of the Moscow audience, openly and unabashedly weeping during the performance. After the concert had ended, the orchestra and I came out of the stage door into the icy street, where people were still waiting for us. A young woman came forward, and, in a mixture of broken English and French, thanked us for the Rachmaninov. Then she gave me a gift, a token of her gratitude to Rachmaninov: one orange, for which she had, without a doubt, queued quite a time that afternoon.

Once Jesus was standing opposite the temple treasury, watching as people dropped their money into the chest. Many rich people were giving large sums. Presently there came a poor widow who dropped in two tiny coins, together worth a farthing. He called his disciples to him. 'I tell you this,' he said: 'this poor widow has given more than any of the others; for those others who have given had more than enough, but she, with less than enough, has given all that she had to live on.'

(Mark 12:41–44, NEB)

Make no mistake, my friends. All good giving, every perfect gift, comes from above, from the Father of the lights of heaven. With him there is no variation, no play of passing shadows. Of his set purpose, by declaring the truth, he gave us birth to be a kind of firstfruits of his creatures.

(James 1:16–18, NEB)

Father, thank you for an orange, an ordinary orange, a very special orange, a sacramental orange.

Father, thank you for two tiny coins, ordinary coins, very special coins, sacramental coins.

They point to something far deeper – warm, firm, gracious, and grateful hearts.

Father, help us to catch something of this fineness of spirit in our living and giving. Amen.

Music-makers of the world unite!

(The Rt. Hon. Edward Heath, President of the International Festival of Youth Orchestras and the Performing Arts, wrote the following on the occasion of the 1980 Festival in Aberdeen. Participating groups came from America, Australia, Canada, Colombia, Czechoslovakia, Denmark, Eire, England, Hong Kong, Peru, Scotland, Switzerland, Taiwan and West Germany.)

I am confident that this year's International Festival of Youth Orchestras and the Performing Arts will be as usual a great success. All those involved in the Festival owe an enormous debt to those who have made it possible, and in particular to the host city of Aberdeen.

At a time of growing international tensions it is good to know that young people from five continents can come together to make music in peace and harmony.

I extend my best wishes to performers and audiences alike. I hope that you will all take away with you the happiest of memories.

But in the last days it shall come to pass, that the mountain of the house of the Lord shall be established in the top of the mountains, and it shall be exalted above the hills; and people shall flow unto it.

And many nations shall come, and say, Come, and let us go up to the mountain of the Lord, and to the house of the God of Jacob; and he will teach us of his ways, and we will walk in his paths: for the law shall go forth of Zion, and the word of the Lord from Jerusalem.

And he shall judge among many people, and rebuke strong nations afar off; and they shall beat their swords into plowshares, and their spears into pruning-hooks: nation shall not lift up a sword against nation, neither shall they learn war any more.

(Micah 4:1–3, AV)

How blest are the peacemakers;
God shall call them his sons.

(Matthew 5:9, NEB)

Father, an International Festival of Music points us, in its own way, towards the ideal of peace. But when we look out at our world we can see anything but peace. Too often there is suspicion, animosity, violence, and bloodshed.

Father, before we are too ready to blame all and sundry, we admit that often the pulsating heat of our own anger has made us say and do things which have all added to the sum total of dissension and discord.

Forgive us.

Save us from becoming dispirited and discouraged. And number us not permanently amongst the pundits of pessimism. But give us a sensible outlook and the integrity of mind to be apostles of perspective, so that we can seek to gather together, in a true vision of life, the bad and the evil, but, beyond them, and even in the midst of them, the many flash-points of hope and justice and the invaluable possibilities of good.

Give us faith and courage to believe that with you the silent stars are strongly set for the everlasting right. Buttress our idealism. Get us doing, in our own ways and in our own situations, the sort of constructive things that make for worthwhile peace. Help us to build bridges of understanding so that men and women of fundamentally different attitudes and opinions, can learn to live together amicably and with dignity.

Father,
Bless the peace makers;
And the peace keepers.
We ask this in your Son's name.
Amen.

All their goods to the poor

Everything Wendy and Alan Weaver have bought for their home since they were married two years ago was auctioned in a street at Shrewsbury yesterday to buy food and medical supplies for Bangladesh.

Their two-room flat was left bare apart from a double bed and a carpet.

The couple's £210 colour television fetched £120, an automatic washing machine went for £70 and hi-fi equipment for £40. Wendy's four paintings raised £2.60.

'The total will not be far short of the £500 they were hoping to raise,' said Major Denis Pursell, a retired auctioneer and former Mayor of Shrewsbury, who conducted the auction.

Wendy (18), a shop assistant, and Alan (29), a salesman, decided on the auction after watching a television documentary about conditions in Bangladesh.

'The programme moved us so deeply we lay awake wondering how to help,' said Wendy. 'We have no savings so we decided to sell everything we had, except the bed. We must have somewhere to sleep.'

Since they decided on the auction the Weavers have received more than £130 from people all over Britain and a £25 cheque from their mayor, Councillor Thomas Ryder. This money is for Bangladesh as well.

'Now that we have nothing left we shall start rebuilding our home again,' Wendy said after the last lot had been auctioned. 'It'll probably take two years to get back to where we were, but at least we have jobs, food to eat and a roof over our heads.'

(From *The Scotsman*)

A man of the ruling class put this question to him: 'Good Master, what must I do to win eternal life?' Jesus said to him, 'Why do you call me good? No one is good except God alone. You know the commandments: "Do not commit adultery; do not murder; do not steal; do not give false evidence; honour your father and mother." ' The man answered, 'I have kept all these since I was a boy.' On hearing this Jesus said, 'There is still one thing lacking: sell everything you have and distribute to the poor, and you will have riches in heaven; and come, follow me.' At these words his heart sank; for he was a very rich man.

(Luke 18:18–23, NEB)

Jesus was at Bethany, in the house of Simon the Leper. As he sat at table, a woman came in carrying a small bottle of very costly perfume, oil of pure nard. She broke it open and poured the oil over his head. Some of those present said to one another angrily, 'Why this waste? The perfume might have been sold for thirty pounds and the money given to the poor'; and they turned upon her with fury. But Jesus said, 'Let her alone. Why must you make trouble for her? It is a fine thing she has done for me. You have the poor among you always, and you can help them whenever you like; but you will not always have me. She has done what lay in her power; she is beforehand with anointing my body for burial. I tell you this: wherever in all the world the Gospel is proclaimed, what she has done will be told as her memorial.'

(Mark 14:3–9, NEB)

Entering Jericho he made his way through the city. There was a man there named Zacchaeus; he was superintendent of taxes and very rich. He was eager to see what Jesus looked like; but, being a little man, he could not see him for the crowd. So he ran on ahead and climbed a sycamore-tree in order to see him, for he was to pass that way. When Jesus came to the place, he looked up and said, 'Zacchaeus, be quick and come down; I must come and stay with you today.' He climbed down as fast as he could and welcomed him gladly. At this there was a general murmur of disapproval. 'He has gone in', they said, 'to be the guest of a sinner.' But Zacchaeus stood there and said to the Lord, 'Here and now, sir, I give half my possessions to charity; and if I have cheated anyone, I am ready to repay him four times over.' Jesus said to him, 'Salvation has come to this house today! – for this man too is a son of Abraham, and the Son of Man has come to seek and save what is lost.'

(Luke 19:1–10, NEB)

Instruct those who are rich in this world's goods not to be proud, and not to fix their hopes on so uncertain a thing as money, but upon God, who endows us richly with all things to enjoy. Tell them to hoard a wealth of noble actions by doing good, to be ready to give away and to share, and so acquire a treasure which will form a good foundation for the future. Thus they will grasp the life which is life indeed.

(1 Timothy 6:7–19, NEB)

May the plea of the needy not fall on selfish ears.
Help us heed it, Father.
Let there be vision and courage in the different ways
in which we respond.
We ask this in the name of your Son, who gave all of
himself, for us. Amen.

The little shadow

What is life? It is the flash of a firefly in the night. It is the breath of a buffalo in the winter time. It is the little shadow that runs across the grass and loses itself in the sunset.

(Reported last words of Crowfoot, the Blackfoot Orator, 1821–90.)

Lord, let me know my end
    and the number of my days;
    tell me how short my life must be.
I know thou hast made my days a mere span long,
    and my whole life is nothing in thy sight.
    Man, though he stands upright, is but a puff of
      wind,
    he moves like a phantom;
    the riches he piles up are no more than vapour,
    he does not know who will enjoy them.

(Psalm 39:4–6, NEB)

When I look up at thy heavens, the work of thy
   fingers,
   the moon and the stars set in their place by thee,
   what is man that thou shouldst remember him,
   mortal man that thou shouldst care for him?
Yet thou has made him little less than a god,
   crowning him with glory and honour.
   Thou makest him master over all thy creatures;
   thou has put everything under his feet:
   all sheep and oxen, all the wild beasts,
   the birds in the air and the fish in the sea,
   and all that moves along the paths of ocean.
O Lord our sovereign,
   how glorious is thy name in all the earth!

(Psalm 8:3–9, NEB)

How fearfully and wonderfully we have been made!
Father, life is your greatest gift. Thank you, above
   all, for the brilliant, unsullied, and incisive life of
   your Son, Jesus Christ.
Help us never to lose sight of the worthwhileness of
   life. And grant that we, with our own little local
   lives, can still be disciples of simple significance
   in the world in which we live, and work, and love.
We ask this for your Son's sake. Amen.

From no – to yes

(Patrick O'Donovan, in an article on the work of the Telephone Samaritans, enumerates the different rules of conduct incumbent on all Samaritans when faced by the sudden cry for help at the end of a telephone.)

The prohibitions are eloquent. There are ten.
1. You do not probe into a client's problems.
2. You do not accept confidences that you cannot tell your director.
3. You do not break promises.
4. You do not give or lend money.
5. You do not allow yourself to be shocked.
6. You do not discuss the problems of clients with other callers.
7. You do not give telephone numbers or addresses (your own included) without permission.
8. You do not proffer advice.
9. You do not say, 'Pull yourself together.'
10. You do not talk religion unless you are asked to do so.

God spoke, and these were his words:

I am the Lord your God who brought you out of Egypt, out of the land of slavery.

1. You shall have no other god to set against me.
2. You shall not make a carved image for yourself.
3. You shall not make wrong use of the name of the Lord your God.
4. Remember to keep the sabbath day holy.
5. Honour your father and your mother.
6. You shall not commit murder.
7. You shall not commit adultery.
8. You shall not steal.
9. You shall not give false evidence against your neighbour.
10. You shall not covet.

(Exodus 20:1–17, abridged, NEB)

Keep out of debt altogether, except that perpetual debt of love which we owe one another. The man who loves his neighbour has obeyed the whole Law in regard to his neighbour. For the commandments, "Thou shalt not commit adultery", "Thou shalt not kill", "Thou shalt not steal", "Thou shalt not covet" and all other commandments are summed up in this one saying: "Thou shalt love thy neighbour as thyself." Love hurts nobody: therefore love is the answer to the Law's commands.

(Romans 13:8–10, JBP)

Then one of the lawyers, who had been listening to these discussions and had noted how well he answered, came forward and asked him, 'Which commandment is first of all?' Jesus answered, 'The first is, "Hear, O Israel: the Lord our God is the only Lord; love the Lord your God with all your heart, with all your soul, with all your mind, and with all your strength." There is no other commandment greater than these.'

(Mark 12:28–31, NEB)

This is my commandment: love one another, as I have loved you.

(John 15:12, NEB)

Jesus Christ, the Son of God, whom Sylvanus, Timothy and I have preached to you, is himself no doubtful quantity, he is the divine "yes". Every promise of God finds its affirmative in him, and through him can be said the final amen, to the glory of God. We owe our position in Christ to this God of positive promise.

(2 Corinthians 1:19–21, JBP)

Father,
help us to see
the ultimate secret of life
is not in the negative,
but in the Positive.

The sensitivity of a butterfly

(Gerald Moore, the Unashamed Accompanist, by dint of his playing, accompanying, writing, and lecturing, has done an immeasurable amount to give the piano accompanist a distinctive and honoured position long over-due in the musical world. Here is a shrewd insight from that happy little book of his – Farewell Recital.*)*

The truth is a successful painter, musician, sculptor, writer, actor has to have the sensitivity of a butterfly coupled, if he hopes to survive, with the hide of a rhinoceros.

(Jesus said) Look, I send you out like sheep among wolves; be wary as serpents, innocent as doves.

(Matthew 10:16, NEB)

Grant us, good Lord, in our living, that very special mixture of delicacy of touch, and toughness of spirit. We ask this in the name of him, who was the very incarnation of strength and gentleness, Jesus Christ.

Ambrose*

(Eberhard Bethge in his outstanding and definitive biography of his former friend and fellow-pastor Dietrich Bonhoeffer – Dietrich Bonhoeffer – Theologian: Christian: Contemporary, *tells of a most significant comment which Bonhoeffer made on his second visit to Switzerland in the late summer of 1941 – four years before he was executed by the Nazi regime for his implication in an abortive plot to overthrow Hitler.)*

Bonhoeffer did not visit Zurich till the second half of his four weeks' stay in freedom. It was probably in the first half when there occurred that conversation which Visser 't Hooft reported immediately after the war, and which produced an unforgettable remark. One evening with Courvoisier, d'Espine, and others, Visser 't Hooft asked: 'What do you really pray for in the present situation?', to which Bonhoeffer is said to have answered: 'If you want to know, I pray for the defeat of my country, for I think that is the only possibility of paying for all the suffering that my country has caused in the world.'

That was a statement that people did not like to hear reproduced in post-war Germany, but whose essential content can hardly be denied, whatever the actual wording may have been. It shows, above all, how absurd and extraordinary the situation was under Hitler, when the true patriot had to speak unpatriotically to show his patriotism. It is a re-action that defied normal feelings in normal times; and it may be a good thing that it is handed down without defence or explanation, so that one comes up against it and relives the incredible happenings of those days. It is abundantly true that the best people of that time had constantly in their minds that they must wish for Germany's defeat to put an end to the injustice.

*In the Maria Regina Martyrum Church in West Berlin, a church dedicated to all the Christians who gave their lives for the freedom of religion and conscience in the period 1933 to 1945, there are five bronze bells. The fifth bell is called the Ambrose bell. It is in E flat. It weighs 683 lbs. On it is the inscription: 'Yet I have to act and to prefer God to the emperor.'

Jeremiah said to Zedekiah, 'These are the words of the Lord the God of Hosts, the God of Israel: If you go our and surrender to the officers of the king of Babylon, you shall live and this city shall not be burnt down; you and your family shall live. But if you do not surrender to the officers of the king of Babylon, the city shall fall into the hands of the Chaldaeans, and they shall burn it down, and you will not escape them.'

(Jeremiah 38:17, 18, NEB)

A number of Pharisees and men of Herod's party were sent to trap him with a question. They came and said, 'Master, you are an honest man, we know, and truckle to no one, whoever he may be; you teach in all honesty the way of life that God requires. Are we or are we not permitted to pay taxes to the Roman Emperor? Shall we pay or not?' He saw how crafty their question was, and said, 'Why are you trying to catch me out? Fetch me a silver piece, and let me look at it.' They brought one, and he said to them, 'Whose head is this, and whose inscription?' 'Caesar's', they replied. Then Jesus said, 'Pay Caesar what is due to Caesar, and pay God what is due to God.' And they heard him with astonishment.

(Mark 12:13–17, NEB)

Every Christian ought to obey the civil authorities, for all legitimate authority is derived from God's authority, and the existing authority is appointed under God. To oppose authority then is to oppose God, and such opposition is bound to be punished.

(Romans 13:1, 2, JBP)

Peter replied for himself and the apostles: 'We must obey God rather than men.'

(Acts 5:29, NEB)

Father, the ultimate allegiance – to whom?
To our kith and kin? To the powers that be?
Our country, right or wrong?
Or is it – or can it only be – to you!

A man's very soul

Electromagnetic radiation of wavelength (is) from about 10− metres downwards. This type of radiation was discovered by Wilhelm Conrad Roentgen in 1895 . . .

X-Rays have a very high penetrating power compared with that of electromagnetic waves of longer wavelength; and this penetrating power increases as the wavelength of the X-Rays is reduced, i.e. as the energy of the X-Rays is increased. The energy of an X-Ray photon is directly proportional to its frequency and therefore inversely proportional to its wavelength. Low energy X-Rays generated at say 20 kilovolts will penetrate a thin sheet of metal foil which would completely block off visible light. Very high energy X-Rays, generated at 10 to 20 million volts, will penetrate a substantial thickness. X-Rays have a powerful ionizing effect, and this provides one means for their detection . . .

Apart from the theoretical interest of X-Rays in connection with the structure of atoms, and their practical value as a tool for scientific research, there is an important application in medicine, both diagnostic and therapeutic . . .

In diagnosis the penetrating power, which allows X-Ray photographs of internal organs to be taken, has been used since very soon after X-Rays were discovered. Therapy depends upon the ionizing power, which can be used in the treatment of abnormal growths.

('X-Rays', from *The New Caxton Encyclopedia*)

Search me, O God, and know my heart: try me, and know my thoughts:
And see if there be any wicked way in me, and lead me in the way everlasting.

(Psalm 139: 23, 24, AV)

The Lord shines into a man's very soul, searching out his inmost being.

(Proverbs 20:27, NEB)

Then they arrested (Jesus) and marched him off to the High Priest's house. Peter followed at a distance, and sat down among some people who had lighted a fire in the middle of the courtyard and were sitting round it. A maid-servant saw him sitting there in the firelight, peered into his face and said,
"This man was with him too."
But he denied it and said,
"I don't know him, girl!"

A few minutes later someone else noticed Peter, and said,

"You're one of these men too."

But Peter said,

"Man, I am not!"

Then about an hour later someone else insisted,

"I am convinced this fellow was with him. Why, he is a Galilean!"

"Man," returned Peter, "I don't know what you're talking about."

And immediately, while he was still speaking, the cock crew. The Lord turned his head and *looked straight at Peter*, and into his mind flashed the words that the Lord had said to him . . . "You will disown me three times before the cock crows today." And he went outside and wept bitterly.

(Luke 22: 54–62, JBP)

For the Word that God speaks is alive and active; it cuts more keenly than any two-edged sword: it strikes through to the place where soul and spirit meet, to the innermost intimacies of a man's being: it exposes the very thoughts and motives of a man's heart. No creature has any cover from the sight of God; everything lies naked and exposed before the eyes of him with whom we have to do.

(Hebrews 4:12, 13, JBP)

Father, we know that, under the gentle but penetrating illumination of Christ, we cannot hide from you. You know us as we really are, with

    our ordinariness and our uniqueness;
    our weaknesses and our strengths;
    our shortsightedness and our visions of faith;
    our qualities and our defects;
    our generosities and our withdrawals.

Father, help us to see that all these are not so much a contradiction of ourselves, but more simply and profoundly, aspects of what we comprehensively are.

Grant us your forgiveness.
And your encouragement.
And guide us in the everlasting ways.
Amen.

DAY 21

Tit for tat?

(Meyer Parry has made a pilot study of behaviour in the driving situation. The result, Aggression on the Road, *makes disconcerting reading. Mr Parry makes very pertinent observations on what happens when a normal person steps into a car and becomes a different breed – the motorist! It all seems to add up to the fact that 'Behaviour not generally tolerated in everyday life is accepted unquestioningly as being a part of motoring.'*

Here is part of an interview Meyer Parry records that he had with a young motorist who admitted, in a previous questionnaire submitted to him by Parry, that his driving depended on just how he felt at any given moment.)

YOUNG MOTORIST: Well, I admit my driving must be a bit worse when I'm in a bad mood, but not so you would notice.

INTERVIEWER: In what way then?

YOUNG MOTORIST: I suppose it makes me less aware of other traffic and sometimes more angry towards them. If I'm trying to catch up with someone and the car in front is blocking my way by moving slowly I flash my lights or use the horn or something like that – I suppose you could say I was less considerate when I'm in a bad mood, but this is only when I'm chasing another driver.

INTERVIEWER: Usually because of a rude sign? Is it necessary to retaliate?

YOUNG MOTORIST: I think it is, I don't believe in turning the other cheek. I don't make rude signs myself, so the only way to pay someone back who does it to me is to knock some manners into him. I feel quite justified in doing that.

Wherever hurt is done, you shall give life for life, eye for eye, tooth for tooth, hand for hand, foot for foot, burn for burn, bruise for bruise, wound for wound.

(Exodus 21:24, NEB)

(Jesus said) You have learned they were told, 'Eye for eye, tooth for tooth'. But what I tell you is this: Do not set yourself against the man who wrongs you. If someone slaps you on the right cheek, turn and offer him your left. If a man wants to sue you for your shirt, let him have your coat as well. If a man in authority makes you go one mile, go with him two. Give when you are asked to give; and do not turn your back on a man who wants to borrow.

(Matthew 5:38–42, NEB)

Don't allow yourself to be overpowered by evil. Take the offensive – overpower evil with good!

(Romans 12:21, JBP)

To sum up: be one in thought and feeling, all of you; be full of brotherly affection, kindly and humble-minded. Do not repay wrong with wrong, or abuse with abuse; on the contrary, retaliate with blessing, for a blessing is the inheritance to which you yourselves have been called.

(1 Peter 3: 8, 9, NEB)

And a prayer, written on a scrap of paper by a concentration camp inmate at Ravensbruck, and found after the camp was liberated, tells its own story of how the steel of a profoundly creative forgiveness was forged.

O Lord, remember not only the men and women of good will but also those of ill will. But do not only remember all the suffering they have inflicted on us. Remember the fruits we bought, thanks to this suffering. Our comradeship, our loyalty, our humility, our courage, our generosity, the greatness of heart which has grown out of all this, and when they come to judgement, let all the fruits that we have borne be their forgiveness.

The quiet style

(Colin Cowdrey reminisces in his autobiography
M.C.C. – The Autobiography of a Cricketer.)

At home, sometimes I sit in my armchair and see
some of the triumphs glowing in the blazing log
fire.

. . . I think of the life of Colin Cowdrey sometimes, almost as if it were not me at all. I have been
a cricketer but so many waves have swept me into
other crevices of life, bringing with them privi-
leges, honours, hard work, pleasant people, bores
occasionally and few truly private moments outside
my own home.

. . . I owe it entirely to cricket that I should be
invited to be the Voice of the Layman for ten
minutes in Coventry Cathedral; the Prime
Minister's guest at Chequers for dinner when he
entertained a visiting Australian Prime Minister,
and to lunch with the Queen and Prince Philip at
Buckingham Palace. . . . These, and many other
links, have made it a full life, extending way
beyond the confines of the cricket field.

. . . It is a full, busy life, though I am not the
extrovert showman who happily wallows in the
public eye. Indeed, I have always admired the

unobtrusive touch. I shall never forget a game of golf I once played. My partner in a foursome, a tall, gentle man who introduced himself as Roger Wethered arrived at the tee. He puffed away on a pipe, wore a quiet country suit. There were others there with flashy trousers and huge sets of gleaming clubs. My partner carried a small bag containing a few irons and two woods. He stroked his way around that course quite effortlessly with an occasional word to me after I had landed him in bush or bunker. "Well played, Colin, so nearly a good one." He was fifty-five then, but had been one of our greatest golfers. That quiet style has always seemed to me to be the right way to carry one's talents.

Here is my servant, whom I uphold,
my chosen one in whom I delight,
I have bestowed my spirit upon him,
and he will make justice shine on the nations.
He will not call out or lift his voice high,
or make himself heard in the open street.
He will not break a bruised reed,
or snuff out a smouldering wick;
he will make justice shine on every race,
never faltering, never breaking down,
he will plant justice on earth,
while coasts and islands wait for his teaching.

(Isaiah 42:1–4, NEB)

(Jesus said) Be careful not to make a show of your religion before men; if you do, no reward awaits you in your Father's house in heaven.

Thus, when you do some act of charity, do not announce it with a flourish of trumpets, as the hypocrites do in synagogue and in the streets to win admiration from men. I tell you this: they have their reward already. No; when you do some act of charity, do not let your left hand know what your right is doing; your good deed must be secret, and your Father who sees what is done in secret will reward you.

Again, when you pray, do not be like the hypocrites; they love to say their prayers standing up in synagogue and at the street-corners, for everyone to see them. I tell you this: they have their reward already. But when you pray, go into a room by yourself, shut the door, and pray to your Father who is there in the secret place; and your Father who sees what is secret will reward you.

(Matthew 6:1–6, NEB)

Act rightly,
Act quietly.
And let the kindred spirits of sincerity, selflessness and integrity be more and more ours.

21/9/93.

It's teamwork that counts!

Climbing with companions creates a wonderfully close relationship, of co-operation and sharing, which is rarely found in everyday life. To tackle a hard climb is a test of each individual's intellect, experience, will, guts, and skill. But each is dependent on the other; not only for achievement, but for mutual security and survival.

This is the quintessence of teamwork, in which each is playing an equal part, and all have complete confidence in one another.

(Sir John Hunt, leader of the first successful ascent of Everest in 1953.)

For Christ is like a single body with its many limbs and organs, which, many as they are, together make up one body.

. . . But God has combined the various parts of the body, giving special honour to the humbler parts, so that there might be no sense of division in the body, but that all its organs might feel the same concern for one another. If one organ suffers, they all suffer together. If one flourishes, they all rejoice together.

Now you are Christ's body, and each of you a limb or organ of it.

(1 Corinthians 12:12, 24–27, NEB)

Two are better than one; they receive a good reward for their toil, because, if one falls, the other can help his companion up again; but alas for the man who falls alone with no partner to help him up. And, if two lie side by side, they keep each other warm; but how can one keep warm by himself?

(Ecclesiastes 4:9–11, NEB)

Carry each other's burdens and so live out the law of Christ.

(Galatians 6:2, JBP)

For everyone has his own proper burden to bear.

(Galatians 6:5, NEB)

Lord, thank you for our blessed and basic inter-dependence in life. Thank you also for the strength of the independent spirit. We know it's the natural thing in preferring to carry rather than be carried. Help us to know when we have to rely on the advice and assistance of others – and when we have to go it alone. Help us to get the balance right. And help us to see that we can have separateness, without separation.

Help us above all to know that ultimately, like your Son Jesus Christ, we depend on you, Lord. And it is that dependability which gives us purpose and peace. Amen.

A fragile existence

(In Albert Camus' book La Peste – The Plague – *celebrations at the end of the book mark the return to normality of the town of Oran and her citizens in Algeria after the ravages of a terrible plague which had lasted for ten long grim months and had claimed many thousands of lives. But Dr. Rieux, who had lived through it all and who had tirelessly fought the plague with all the professional skill at his command, is under no delusions as to the reality of the situation. He has his own sombre thoughts on the continuing precariousness of the human predicament.)*

From the dark harbour soared the first rocket of the firework display organized by the municipality, and the two acclaimed it with a longdrawn sigh of delight. Cottard, Tarrou, the men and the women Rieux had loved and lost – all alike, dead or guilty, were forgotten. Yes, the old fellow had been right; these people were 'just the same as ever'. But this was at once their strength and their innocence, and it was on this level, beyond all grief, that Rieux could feel himself at one with them. And it was in the midst of shouts rolling against the terrace wall in massive waves that waxed in volume and duration while cataracts of coloured fires fell thicker through the darkness, that Dr. Rieux resolved to compile this chronicle, so that he should not be one of those who hold their peace but should bear witness in favour of those plague-stricken people; so that some memorial of the injustice and outrage done them might endure; and to state quite simply what we learn in a time of pestilence: that there are more things to admire in men than to despise.

None the less, he knew that the tale he had to tell could not be one of a final victory. It could be only the record of what had had to be done, and what assuredly would have to be done again in the never-ending fight against terror and its relentless onslaughts, despite their personal afflictions, by all who, while unable to be saints but refusing to bow down to pestilences, strive their utmost to be healers.

And, indeed, as he listened to the cries of joy rising from the town, Rieux remembered that such joy is always imperilled. He knew what those jubilant crowds did not know but could have learned from books: that the plague bacillus never dies or disappears for good; that it can lie dormant for years in furniture and linen-chests; that it bides its time in bedrooms, cellars, trunks, and bookshelves; and that perhaps the day would come when, for the bane and the enlightenment of men, it roused up its rats again and sent them forth to die in a happy city.

Again I saw that under the sun the race is not to the swift, nor the battle to the strong, nor bread to the wise, nor riches to the intelligent, nor favour to the men of skill; but time and chance happen to them all. For man does not know his time. Like fish which are taken in an evil net, and like birds which are caught in a snare, so the sons of men are snared at an evil time, when it suddenly falls upon them.

(Ecclesiastes 9:11, 12, RSV)

And what is faith? Faith gives substance to our hopes, and makes us certain of realities we do not see.

(Hebrews 11:1, NEB)

Lord, can we progress
In terms of our own individual integrity,
From the perceptive pessimism of the preacher,
On through the rigorous realism of a Rieux,
To a firmer faith in you?

Lord, we have faith,
But help us where our faith falls short.

Operation icecube

Little Neil Bingham was alive last night . . . thanks to Operation Icecube.

The two-year-old was saved by an army of Good Samaritans who answered a hospital's 3 a.m. emergency plea: "Bring us your ice."

Neil's condition was deteriorating rapidly as he lay in an oxygen tent, a victim of the killer illness, croup. ✳ P.T.O.

The doctors had to get his raging temperature down – but their ice-making equipment was broken.

So they rang a radio station in Birmingham and asked for the appeal to be broadcast.

Within minutes scores of listeners had emptied their fridges and were heading for Wordsley Hospital, near Dudley, Worcester.

One old couple walked two miles from their home, clutching a bucketful of ice.

And a lorry driver who was delivering to hotels arrived with a 5 cwt. block of it.

The ice was packed into Neil's oxygen tent – and last night he was sitting up, chatting to nursing staff.

Nursing Officer Michael Carrier said: "The people who answered our appeal were absolutely marvellous. We can't pay tribute enough to them.

The ice was vital to reduce the boy's temperature and also the temperature in the oxygen tent itself. In the end we had a lot more ice than we really needed."

Neil's dad, 29-year-old welder Terry Bingham, said: "It was a nightmare. My wife Jenny and I had been called in the early morning because of the doctor's fears. We want to say thank you to everyone who rallied round."

The appeal was put out over the air by DJ Dave Barber, who runs an all-night record and chat show.

He said: "I'm knocked out by the response. This sort of reaction to a human crisis is one of the great things about running a late radio show." (Note – Croup results in inflammation of the throat, uncontrollable coughing and very high temperatures. Victims can choke to death.)

(Paul Connew in the *Daily Mirror*)

I tell you this: anything you did for one of my brothers here, however humble, you did for me.

(Matthew 25:40, NEB)

So often respectably unmindful of others, and not really wanting to be involved, we exercise the negative virtue of keeping ourselves to ourselves.
And then comes the emergency.
And that other positive side to our human nature stands forward. And we begin to mine again the rich seams of our own original goodness; for that – thanks be to God!

DAY 26

A kind of rebirth

(*In 1973 Scotland created the Special Unit at Bar-
linnie Prison, Glasgow, as a courageous and far-
seeing experiment in the treatment of long-term and
potentially violent prisoners. The experiment em-
braces a more psychological and tolerant approach to
the prisoners. Here, Jimmy Boyle, who is serving a
life sentence for murder and attempted murder and
who was one of the first prisoners to be part of the
Special Unit, recounts in his book,* A Sense of Freedom, *just how he felt about the challenge of the new
experimental unit.*)

Although I had decided to have a go in helping to
get the unit off the ground, it didn't mean that all my
problems were solved – far from it. Accepting responsibility was the crucial one as that entailed
making decisions, having to consider others, and
looking at my own life in relation to others. These
were things that I had to learn as I had come from a
world where decision making was taken out of my
hands. If I had wanted a cup of water, the toilet,
soap, etc. etc. then I had had to ask for it. Now I was
having to cope with not only these questions but to
think in terms of other people and it was pretty
frightening. In order to be able to do this and to

77

understand others I had to find out more about myself. This is what made the Special Unit such a tough place to live in – the fact that every single one of us had to look at himself, warts and all, probably for the first time in his life. In the general penal system one could be next door to a person for years and think that one knew him, but all one really knows is the superficial "front" that that person wanted one to know. I had known Ben and Larry off and on for fifteen years in Approved School, Borstal, and prisons but I was to find that they were comparative strangers to me till the point where we entered the Unit. Only then was I able to get to know them in depth; and they me, I suppose. I had been in solitary in Inverness with them and it was smaller than the Special Unit, but it was the general penal system structure that existed there and this was the difference, as the Unit allowed the individual to be himself. There lay the problem, as many of us, staff and inmates, began to realise we really didn't know who we were. I personally felt that the best way for me to adjust to this new way was to look on it as a rebirth; it is true to say that I was experiencing lots of things for the first time in my life.

There was one of the Pharisees named Nico-demus, a member of the Jewish Council, who came to Jesus by night. 'Rabbi', he said, 'we know that you are a teacher sent by God; no one could perform these signs of yours unless God were with him.' Jesus answered, 'In truth, in very truth I tell you, unless a man has been born over again he cannot see the kingdom of God.' 'But how is it possible', said Nicodemus, 'for a man to be born when he is old? Can he enter his mother's womb a second time and be born?' Jesus answered, 'In truth I tell you, no one can enter the kingdom of God without being born from water and spirit. Flesh can give birth only to flesh; it is spirit that gives birth to spirit. You ought not to be astonished, then, when I tell you that you must be born over again.'

(John 3:1–7, NEB)

. . . for you have finished with the old man and all he did and have begun life as the new man, who is out to learn what he ought to be, according to the plan of God.

(Colossians 3:9b, 10, JBP)

Help us, Lord, to begin to face the truth about our own mistakes and failings. Give us courage to see that it is never too late to start on the work of renovation, so that we can 'be made new in mind and spirit, and put on the new nature of (your) creating' (Ephesians 4:23, 24a, NEB).

A very special offer

(In one of V.S.O.'s most compelling posters chal-lenging young people to give a year of their lives to Voluntary Service Overseas, Karsh of Ottawa, the world-famous photographer, has superbly captured the craggy and indomitable features of Albert Schweitzer in his picture. Underneath is the follow-ing terse challenge,)

YOU WON'T BE THE FIRST LONG-HAIRED IDEALIST TO GO INTO THE JUNGLE AND TEACH HIS SKILLS.

Tradesmen and craftsmen, graduates and teachers, engineers and technicians, agricultural-ists and foresters, medical auxiliaries, librarians and accountants, surveyors and architects, urgently needed for voluntary service overseas. If you would like more information please contact:

Voluntary Service Overseas,
9 Belgrave Square,
London, SW1 8PW   Tel: 01-235 5347/9744

HARD WORK. LONG HOURS. LOW PAY.
THE MOST MEMORABLE YEAR OF YOUR LIFE.

Then (Jesus) called the people to him, as well as his disciples, and said to them, 'Anyone who wishes to be a follower of mine must leave self behind; day after day he must take up his cross, and come with me. Whoever cares for his own safety is lost; but if a man will let himself be lost for my sake, that man is safe.'

(Mark 8:34b; Luke 9:23b, 24, NEB)

Enter by the narrow gate. The gate is wide that leads to perdition, there is plenty of room on the road, and many go that way; but the gate that leads to life is small and the road is narrow, and those who find it are few.

(Matthew 7:13, 14, NEB)

Father, here is the challenge of decision, commitment, and sacrifice.
But here also is the chance to live, and to live abundantly.
Here is the opportunity to begin a journey into faith, hope, and love.
Here is real security!

In honour of the individual

(*In the opening chapter of* Journey *into Russia Laurens van der Post finds, on examination of books and newspapers, that Russian individuality is a very difficult thing to come by. He looks back to 1961 when he had visited East Berlin and recalls the impressions that the Russian War Memorial there had made on him.*)

It was built on top of a vast grave into which some 80,000 Russian dead had been bulldozed. Somehow it seemed to the Russians that their soldiers were collective in death as they had been in life. In the West huge organisations are maintained in all our armies to make certain that after death the individual can be identified, given decent burial in a separate grave and his sacrifice acknowledged with a cross bearing his name, number, date of birth, time and manner of death. But this Russian Memorial implied that these wide differences between the Soviet world and our own were matters that involved not only life but death itself. Climbing up the tiers of steps to the top of the building the depression which this realisation caused in me was increased by the wreaths piled high on the balustrades. It happened on that day to be the anniversary of the battle in which the 80,000 men had been killed and the wreaths were new and their artificial flowers bright. I looked closely at the inscriptions. They too were all official and collective with dedications like: 'The workers of the ship-building yards of Rostock salute the glorious Soviet dead,' or 'The collective farmers of Silesia pay ever-lasting homage, etc. etc.' I looked in vain for some wreath or posy of flowers saying no more than: 'Jack remembered with love from Jill' or 'Bill from his everlasting Mum.' None the less my belief per-sisted that behind the opaque official front there was a man and his humanity to be discovered and honoured, and until this were done no real under-standing between ourselves and the Russians would be possible.

But now this is the word of the Lord,
the word of your creator, O Jacob,
    of him who fashioned you, Israel:
Have no fear; for I have paid your ransom;
I have called you by name and you are my own.

(Isaiah 43:1, NEB)

(Jesus said) Are not sparrows five for twopence? And yet not one of them is overlooked by God. More than that, even the hairs of your head have all been counted. Have no fear; you are worth more than any number of sparrows.

(Luke 12:6, 7, NEB)

Jesus said, 'Mary!'

(John 20:16a, NEB)

Shake the hand of dear Epaenetus, Achaia's first
man to be won for Christ, and of course greet Mary
who has worked so hard for you. A handshake too
for Andronicus and Junias my kinsmen and fellow-
prisoners; they are outstanding men among the
messengers and were Christians before I was.

Another warm greeting for Ampliatus, dear
Christian that he is, and also for Urbanus, who has
worked with me, and dear old Stachys, too.

More greetings from me, please, to:
Apelles, the man who has proved his faith,
The household of Aristobulus,
Herodion, my kinsman,
Narcissus' household, who are Christians.

Remember me to Tryphena and Tryphosa, who
work so hard for the Lord, and to my dear Persis
who has also done great work for him.

Shake the hand of Rufus for me – that splendid
Christian, and greet his mother, who has been a
mother to me too. Greetings to Asyncritus,
Phlegon, Hermes, Patrobas, Hermas and their
Christian group: also to Philologus and Julia,
Nereus and his sister, and Olympas and the
Christians who are with them.

Give each other a hearty handshake all round for
my sake. The greetings of all the churches I am in
touch with come to you with this letter.

(Romans 16:5b–16, JBP)

Father, we thank you for all the unanalysable subtleties that make us what we are. We thank you for the accolade of our different names.

In what can, in so many ways, be an impersonal age, help us always to insist on the worth of the personal dimension. Help us to respect the humanity of others, and not to do anything that would suppress their individuality.

We ask this in the name of your Son, Jesus Christ, Amen.

Rugged perspectives

An hour or so from London the British Airways Shuttle services – SCOTLAND: one of the last great stretches of unmolested countryside in Europe. As oil comes ashore from the North Sea, it is changing but the great sea lochs, the islands and the wild, hushed mountain passes of the Highlands seem timeless.

Scotland for the visitor is a heady mix of tradition and fine sport, wild life and stunning scenery. Golf, fishing and climbing rank with the best in the world. Nowhere can touch it for whisky!

It's a special kind of holiday in Scotland: no one goes for the night life or razzamattazz – but for a sense of romantic history, fresh and rugged perspectives, a purity of nature, the country is an environmentalist's dream.

(From *Great Britain – A summer visitor's guide*, compiled by British Airways.)

Bless the Lord, my soul:
    thou didst fix the earth on its foundation
    so that it never can be shaken;

Thou dost make springs break out in the gullies,
   so that their water runs between the hills.
The wild beasts all drink from them,
the wild asses quench their thirst;
the birds of the air nest on their banks
and sing among the leaves.

From thy high pavilion thou dost water the hills;
the earth is enriched by thy provision.
Thou makest grass grow for the cattle and
   green things for those who toil for man,
bringing bread out of the earth
and wine to gladden men's hearts,
oil to make their faces shine
and bread to sustain their strength.
   The trees of the Lord are green and leafy,
   the cedars of Lebanon which he planted;
the birds build their nests in them,
the stork makes her home in their tops.
High hills are the haunt of the mountain-goat,
and boulders a refuge for the rock-badger.

Countless are the things thou has made, O Lord.
Thou hast made all by thy wisdom;
and the earth is full of thy creatures,
beasts great and small.

(Psalm 104:1a, 5, 10–18, 24, 25a, NEB)

*Let us cherish
the land that we live in,
because it is God-given
and good!*

Kiowa myth

It used to be that the Kiowa (old Red Indian tribe) used only dogs for pack animals. Then one time an old medicine man had a dream in which he saw a strange animal. He was thinking about how he could make it. He took some mud and made a body, covered it with the hair of a prairie dog, gave it the eyes of an eagle, hoofs made from turtle shell, and wings to make it travel faster. But the horse flew away up into the air and did not return. There it remained to bring cyclones. Later the old man made another animal just like the first, but without wings. It was successful. From that time on the Kiowa have had horses.

Then the Lord God formed a man from the dust of the ground and breathed into his nostrils the breath of life. Thus the man became a living creature. . . . Then the Lord God said, 'It is not good for the man to be alone. I will provide a partner for him.' So God formed out of the ground all the wild animals and all the birds of heaven. He brought them to the man to see what he would call them, and whatever the man called each living creature, that was its name. Thus the man gave names to all cattle, to the birds of heaven, and to every wild animal; but for the man himself no partner had yet been found. And so the Lord God put the man into a trance, and while he slept, he took one of his ribs and closed the flesh over the place. The Lord God then built up the rib, which he had taken out of the man, into a woman. He brought her to the man, and the man said:

'Now this, at last –
bone from my bones,
flesh from my flesh! –
this shall be called woman,
for from man was this taken.'

That is why a man leaves his father and mother and is united to his wife, and the two become one flesh.

(Genesis 2:7, 18–24, NEB)

Thank you Father, for the poetry, the richness, and the mystery of biblical myth.
Disarmingly yet shrewdly, it seeks to explain the inexplicable, and to convey what cannot be grasped by the mind of man.
Its earthiness and colour are harnessed for the proclamation of the truth – Your Truth: You care for us – You have faith in us – You love us with an everlasting love.

DAY 31

The inextinguishable hope

(Here is a moving and splendid affirmation of faith from Anne Frank. It's made right at the end of her famous diary – a diary that was kept while she and her family and friends, like many Dutch Jews, went into hiding from the Nazis. From June 1942 to August 1944 the Franks lived high up in a secret annex at 263 Prinsengrad, Amsterdam. A few days after this entry was made in her diary the Franks were betrayed and arrested by the German Security Police. They were sent to Auschwitz Concentration Camp where Anne died in March 1945. The Franks' house in Prinsengrad is now the centre of the Anne Frank Foundation and is dedicated to the Universal Declaration of Human Rights.)

That's the difficulty in these times: ideals, dreams, and cherished hopes rise within us, only to meet the horrible truth and be shattered.

It's really a wonder that I haven't dropped all my ideals because they seem so absurd and impossible to carry out. Yet, I keep them, because in spite of everything I still believe that people are really good at heart. I simply can't build up my hopes on a foundation consisting of confusion, misery, and death. I see the world gradually being turned into a wilderness, I hear the ever-approaching thunder, which will destroy us too, I can feel the sufferings of millions and yet, if I look up into the heavens, I think it will all come right, that this cruelty too will end, and that peace and tranquility will return again.

In the meantime, I must uphold my ideals, for perhaps the time will come when I shall be able to carry them out.

Although the fig-tree does not burgeon,
the vines bear no fruit,
the olive-crop fails,
the orchards yield no food,
the fold is bereft of its flock
    and there are no cattle in the stalls,
yet I will exult in the Lord
    and rejoice in the God of my deliverance.
The Lord God is my strength,
who makes my feet nimble as a hind's
    and sets me to range the heights.

(Habbakuk 3:17–19, NEB)

For I reckon that the sufferings of this present time are not worthy to be compared with the glory which shall be revealed in us.

And we know that all things work together for good to them that love God, to them who are the called according to his purpose.

Who shall separate us from the love of Christ? shall tribulation, or distress, or persecution, or famine, or nakedness, or peril, or sword?

Nay, in all these things we are more than conquerors through him that loved us.

For I am persuaded, that neither death, nor life, nor angels, nor principalities, nor powers, nor things present, nor things to come,

Nor height, nor depth, nor any other creature, shall be able to separate us from the love of God, which is in Christ Jesus our Lord.

(Romans 8:18, 28, 35, 37–39, AV)

Here are words you may trust:
'If we died with him, we shall live with him;
if we endure, we shall reign with him.'

(2 Timothy 2:11, 12a, NEB)

Lord Jesus Christ, no matter how parlous our plight may be, give us the courage to affirm your loving presence and understanding, to the very end of time.

Index of biblical references